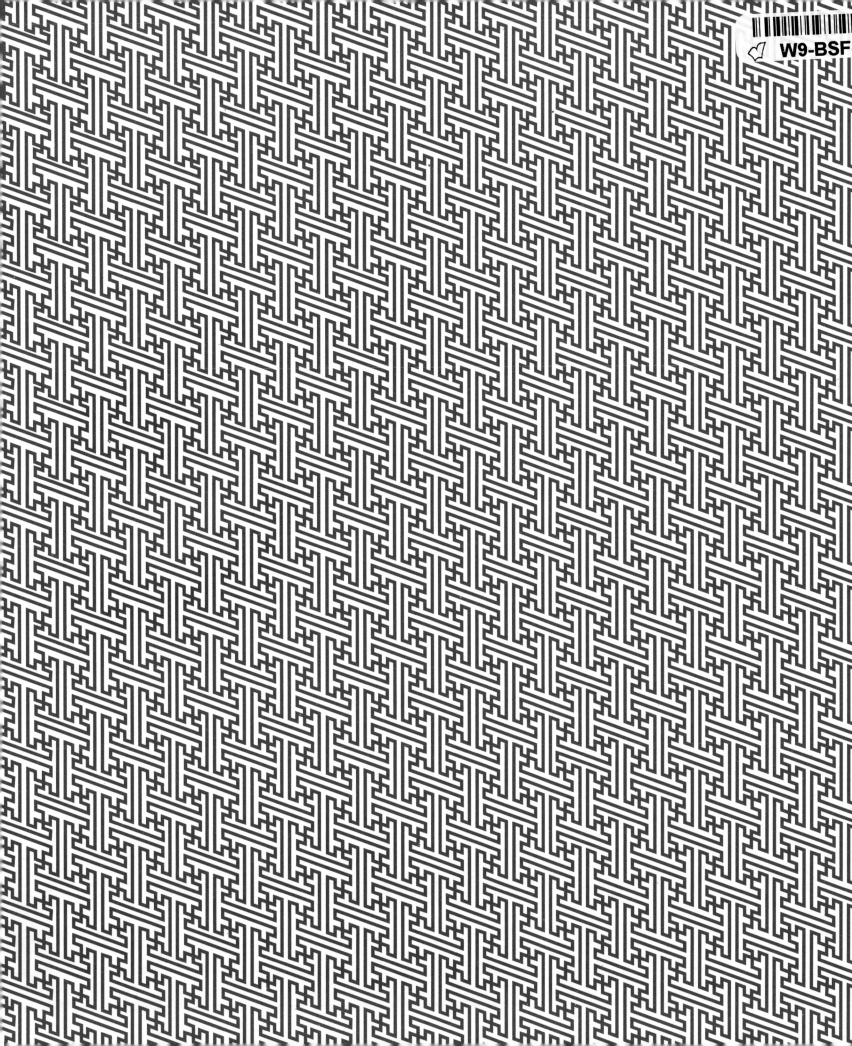

W9-BSF-053

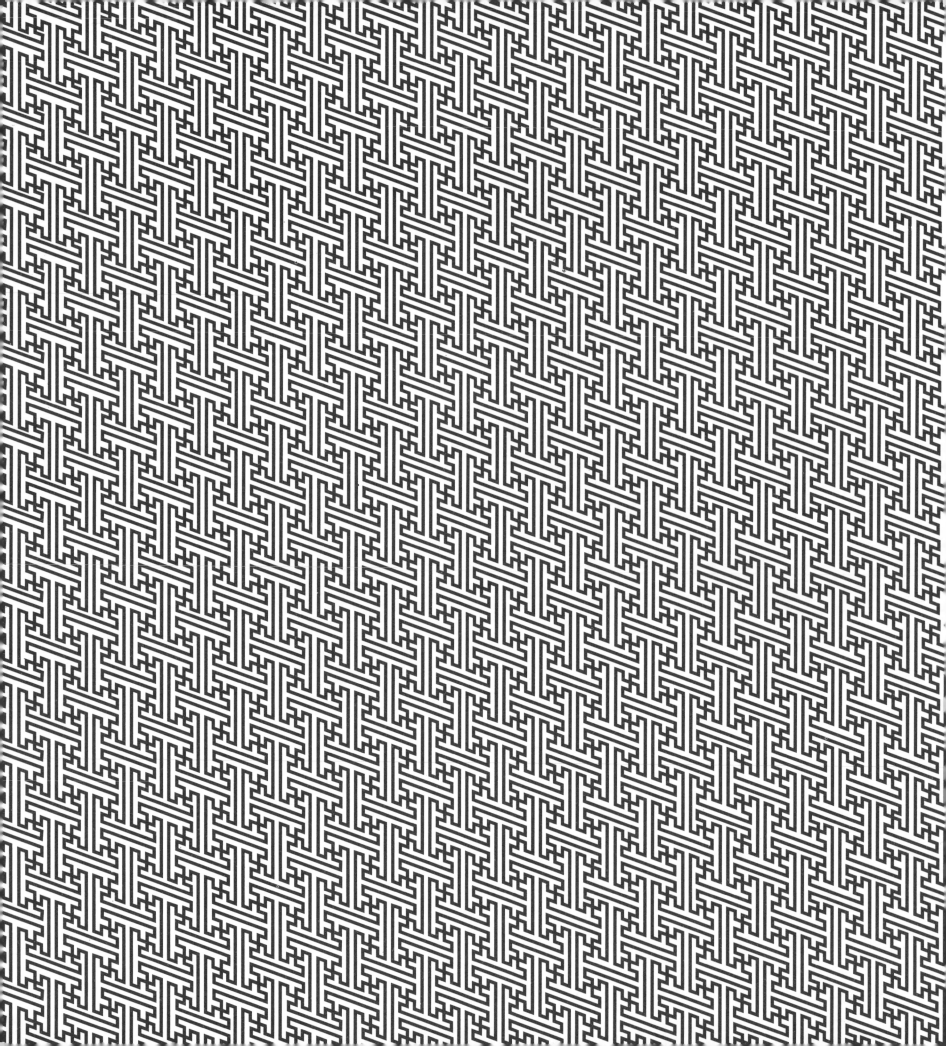

THE LIFE OF A
GEISHA

THE LIFE OF A

GEISHA

ELEANOR UNDERWOOD ❀ FOREWORD BY LIZA DALBY

SMITHMARK

Copyright © 1999 by SMITHMARK Publishers

All rights reserved. No part of this publication may be reproduced,
stored in a retrieval system, or transmitted in any form or by any means,
electronic, mechanical, photocopying, recording or otherwise, without
prior permission of the copyright holders.

SMITHMARK books are available for bulk purchase for sales promotion
and premium use. For details, write or call the manager of special sales,
SMITHMARK Publishers, 115 West 18th Street, New York, NY 10011.

Produced by SMITHMARK PUBLISHERS
115 West 18th Street, New York, NY 10011.

Creative Direction: Kristen Schilo, Gato & Maui Productions
Design: Lynne Yeamans

0-7651-1739-8

Library of Congress Cataloging-in-Publication Data
Underwood, Eleanor.
        The life of a Geisha / Eleanor Underwood : foreword by
    Liza Dalby.
            p.   cm.
        ISBN 0-7651-1739-8 (hc.)
        1. Geishas.   I. Title.
    GT3412.U53   1999   99-30457
    306.74'2'0952--dc21   CIP

Printed and bound in Hong Kong

10 9 8 7 6 5 4 3 2 1

TITLE PAGE: *Shigemasa, late eighteenth century*
OPPOSITE: *Hokkei, early nineteenth century*
PAGE 6: Maiko rinsen *by Tsuchida Bakusen, 1924*

TO MARIANI, FOR HER VIGOR,

VERVE, AND GENEROSITY.

TABLE OF CONTENTS

FOREWORD BY LIZA DALBY

8

INTRODUCTION

10

ALLURING ENTERTAINERS OF OLD

14

THE GOLDEN AGE OF GEISHA

22

PREWAR DECADENCE

30

CHANGES WITH WARTIME

34

THE LIFE OF A GEISHA

40

THE CHARMS OF A GEISHA

46

THE ARTS OF A GEISHA

50

AFTERWORD: GEISHA TODAY

58

GLOSSARY

60

SELECTED BIBLIOGRAPHY

62

CREDITS

62

INDEX

64

FOREWORD

I was twenty-five when my "older sister" Ichiume first brushed the geisha's cold white makeup on my face. She was twenty-one. In the geisha world of Kyoto she was still my senior since she had graduated from the status of *maiko* to that of full-fledged *geiko* the year before. I, of course, had never been a *maiko*. Ichiume had taken on the task of showing this American graduate student the inside perspective of a *geiko* (the Kyoto dialect term for geisha) behind the history, the statistics, and the interviews I had been collecting. Some customers were surprised to find their saké cup filled by an American geisha; and some didn't even notice until the other geisha began to giggle.

I made no secret of the reason behind my transformation into Ichiume's younger sister Ichigiku of Pontochō—I was trying to obtain a deeper understanding of the profession of geisha in order to write my Ph.D. thesis in cultural anthropology. The suggestion that I put on kimono and take my *shamisen* to the teahouses came from the geisha themselves. After I had gotten to know them and they me, they seemed to think I might be able to tell their side of the story—for geisha definitely feel they are misunderstood in the West.

The word "geisha" conjures up a mythically exotic creature in the Western imagination. Fantasy, wishful thinking, and plain misconceptions have been bound together with threads of fact, so that in English to say "geisha" summons a vision of a servile beauty who dotes upon her master's whim, satisfying every desire. Her personality he need not bother about, and she will obligingly melt away like Madame Butterfly rather than disturb him. This fantasy is hard to project on a real woman, but settles quite easily on a mythic one.

Geisha have the odd distinction of being both legendary and real, and this book helps clarify those differences. Myth by nature is monolithic, transcending history and individuals, whereas the reality is a variety of geisha communities in different areas of Japan, status hierarchies among communities in the same city, and of course differences among individual geisha.

This is not to say that geisha are not exotic. These women are more mysterious than they themselves imagine—in Japan as well as outside it, albeit for different reasons. Westerners have a notion that geisha must be experts in the art of subservience in a country like Japan where even ordinary women are supposed to put men first. We infer that the art of pleasing men would mean being even more servile. I myself accepted this myth before I learned better as Ichigiku. To my surprise, I found that the social give and take between geisha and customers in the teahouses of Kyoto was quite comfortable to an American-bred geisha. One must not confuse the general cultural norms of Japanese politeness with subservience. Geisha are among the most outspoken Japanese women I know. Of course they are socially skillful—like a good hostess in America they don't say things that would embarrass a guest. But it became clear to me that Japanese men do not consort with geisha because they crave more subservience. They crave interesting conversation and lively personalities.

We do not have an institution comparable to geisha in modern Western societies. Geisha do not marry, but they often have children. They live in organized professional communities of women. They have affairs with married men, and can form other liaisons at their own discretion. They derive their livelihood from singing, dancing, and chatting with men at banquets. They devote their time to learning and performing traditional forms of music and dance. And they always dress in kimono, but not always the formal costume. In various ways, then, geisha may be like mistresses, waitresses, hostesses, dancers, or performers. If she's not in full dress, can you tell she's a geisha? If you know what to look for, yes.

As Japanese women, the most important social fact about geisha is that they are not wives. These are mutually exclusive categories because of the way women's roles have been traditionally defined in Japan. Wives have always controlled the private sphere of home and children; the profession of geisha, for all its exclusivity, came into existence in a space separate both from the private world of the home and the public one of business. This was the arena where men could socialize. Geisha are by no means the only women who serve this function—they are outnumbered 1000 to 1 by bar hostesses in modern Japan—but this is still one of the two *raisons d'être* of their profession. This is how they differ from wives. What sets them apart from the other women in the entertainment industry is, of course, their *gei*, their devotion to traditional arts.

It's true that their world has undergone many changes—it had to in order to survive. Until the 1920's, when they began to look old-fashioned next to the modern café and dancehall girls, geisha had been society's fashion vanguard. But in the face of modernization and westernization, geisha managed to twist the meaning of their profession in the opposite direction and transform themselves from fashion innovators into curators of tradition. Leaving Western dress to the bar hostesses, geisha turned kimono into their uniform. In this way they found their niche within modern Japan. The experience of oppressed indentureship of Arthur Golden's character Sayuri in his book *Memoirs of a Geisha* no longer occurs, nor does the custom of ritual defloration of a *maiko*, a privilege bestowed on the highest bidder. Yet older geisha still tell such tales of their youth, along with the strict discipline they endured at the hands of their dance and *shamisen* teachers.

"You couldn't do that today," said my geisha mother, "the *maiko* would quit." Arthur Golden accomplished a remarkable feat of imagination when he put himself inside the mind of a geisha and went on to create a compelling personality through the unfolding of events in her larger-than-life saga. Yet in this, Sayuri's story rings true because geisha are still, in fact, larger than life.

Liza Dalby

May 1999

INTRODUCTION

A [geisha is a] girl exquisitely refined in all her ways; her costume a chef-d'oeuvre of decorative art; her looks demure yet arch; her manners restful and self-contained, yet sunny and winsome; her movements gentle and unobtrusive, but musically graceful; her conversation a piquant mixture of feminine inconsequence and sparkling repartée; her list of light accomplishments inexhaustible; her subjective modesty a model, and her objective complacency unmeasured.

–Captain Frank Brinkley, at the turn of the century

Geisha, along with Mt. Fuji and cherry blossoms, have been symbols of Japan to foreigners ever since Japan opened to the West in the 1850s. Who are geisha? We often hear that true geisha (pronounced gay-sha) are not prostitutes—geisha means "arts person"—but instead are highly trained entertainers. Traditionally their appeal *is* based on a highly refined eroticism, but the geisha's sexual favors are not directly for sale and are very difficult to attain. In truth, the answer to the question "who are geisha?" differs both geographically and historically within Japan.

The Western fascination with geisha can be seen in many forms. The 1906 opera Madame Butterfly by Puccini, though not actually about a geisha, probably did the most to create the stereotype of the fragile

ABOVE: *The sacred Mount Fuji was celebrated in the nineteenth century as a symbol of Japan, as seen in this 1830s woodcut print by Hokusai.*

Oriental beauty whom the Westerner loves and then leaves behind. When the post-World War II era brought a renewed fascination with Japan, Shirley MacLaine played a geisha in the 1962 film *My Geisha*. And even Madonna has taken to dressing like a geisha, in her noted post-modern way.

The Japanese themselves have done their part in promoting geisha as symbols of Japan to the rest of the world—geisha have decorated posters advertising Japan ever since Japanese travel posters were first printed. Posters for the first geisha dance spectaculars were written in English as well as in Japanese. Today, many Japanese would concur that geisha represent traditional Japanese feminine virtues, despite the fact that very few Japanese have actually had any personal contact with geisha, since geisha parties are prohibitively expensive.

Arthur Golden's fictional *Memoirs of a Geisha* goes beyond these and other geisha stereotypes and in doing so, brilliantly reveals the fascinating world of a twentieth-century geisha. The book tells the story of a girl named Chiyo who becomes the well-known geisha "Sayuri" in Kyoto's

ABOVE: *Early in the century foreign visitors to Japan could buy postcards featuring geisha and cherry blossoms, both already symbolic of Japan.*

RIGHT: *Two* maiko *display back and side views of their gorgeous attire as they look out toward this Kyoto covered bridge.*

BELOW: *Like the character of Sayuri, many who became geisha were born in poor agricultural or fishing villages before being sold to* oki-ya *houses.*

THE GEISHA OF TATSUMI GOES

WALKING,

BARE WHITE FEET IN BLACK

LACQUERED CLOGS.

IN HER HAORI JACKET, SHE'S THE

PRIDE OF GREAT EDO.

AH, THE HACHIMAN BELL IS

RINGING.

An anonymous ko-uta (geisha song)

high-class geisha district of Gion, taking us through Chiyo's life from a poor fishing-village girl in the 1920s to her final days as the esteemed mistress of a wealthy patron. In its myriad of details and atmospheric color, Golden's book vividly portrays a little known subculture of Japan in the years before and after World War II. It is a convincing portrait of Sayuri's heroic survival: from her early hardships, through adolescent rivalries, to final happiness. With vibrant *ukiyo-e* prints, period photographs, evocative poetry, geisha songs, and text, *The Life of a Geisha* explores and expands upon the world of the geisha that has long intrigued observers around the world.

IS THIS LOVE REALITY
OR A DREAM?
I CANNOT KNOW,
WHEN BOTH REALITY AND DREAMS
EXIST WITHOUT TRULY EXISTING.

Ono no Komachi (Ninth century)

LEFT: *A maiko, framed by the door of a teahouse balcony, gazes out on a pagoda against the Kyoto mountains.*

ABOVE: *Children play on the beach of a fishing village as little Chiyo did, while their mothers scrub the baskets used to dry fish in the sun.*

RIGHT: *Two maiko, holding their kimono up with their left hands, chat on the street of one of the Kyoto hanamachi (geisha quarters).*

FAR RIGHT: *In this ukiyo-e print from the 1850s, Hiroshige depicts travelers on one of Japan's early highways, with Mt. Fuji in the distance.*

WRESTLING AT TOKIO.

LEFT: *A young beauty in casual kimono holds her puppy snugly in a piece of cloth in this turn-of-the-century photo.*

ABOVE: *Sumo wrestlers clap and stamp in a circle for a ceremonious start to the day's bout.*

RIGHT: *Two young charmers share a large rain parasol as they stroll together under a willow.*

BELOW: *Geisha peer through the snow in front of the shrine of Gion in Kyoto in this mid nineteenth-century print by Hiroshige.*

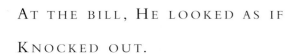

AT THE BILL, HE LOOKED AS IF KNOCKED OUT.

*An anonymous senryū
(Edo-period satirical poem)*

ALLURING ENTERTAINERS OF OLD

Geisha, by that name, have occupied only a short space in the long span of Japanese history. It was only a few hundred years ago that those recognizable today as geisha emerged. However, the geisha "type"—women who entertained and then offered their bodies to men—goes back to earliest times in Japan. Depending on their level of artistry, sensitivity, and intelligence, these women, like geisha later on, could become famous and even powerful, Japanese figures.

The earliest predecessors to geisha were found among the *saburuko* (ones who served) who arose at the end of the seventh century. These women, who were forced to become wanderers as a result of social displacement, traded their sexual favors in order to survive. Among them were talented dancers and singers who were invited into the aristocratic compounds to entertain at gatherings. There is mention of these women in ancient Japanese poetry.

From the twelfth to the fourteenth centuries a new class of courtesans, called *shirabyōshi*, emerged. They were highly accomplished minstrels and dancers who wore white Shinto-style dress and played the drum and fife. Often coming from fallen aristocratic families, they were

OPPOSITE: *The eleventh-century* **The Tale of Genji** *by Murasaki Shikibu epitomized the sensitive ideal of Japanese romance that inspired Edo-period fantasies enacted in the pleasure quarters. This 1896 image of Ukifune is based on a picture by Mitsunoki.*

ABOVE: *A bathhouse scene in summer, by Yoshitoshi in 1883, shows courtesans of Nezu in Tokyo.*

also the result of social upheaval. The names of some of these women have become legendary. Most famous is *Shizuka*, who was the companion of the most beloved warrior of medieval Japan, Yoshitsune. Another, Kamegiku, the concubine of the Emperor Gotoba, was said to have begun a war through spite! Some of the ancient legends, hymns and ballads that their tradition preserved were later taken up by the *Noh* theater.

LIFE IN THE PLEASURE QUARTERS

Saburuko and *shirabyōshi* were only antecedents to geisha in that they were female entertainers who were free with their bodies. But geisha could not have arisen without the later culture of the *yūjo* (courtesans), the hot-house flowers who lived in *yūkaku*, the walled-in pleasure quarters.

The term "pleasure quarters" was ironic in some ways. Around 1600 the walled-in quarters were actually instituted as a form of incarceration. They were established when the new Tokugawa regime (named after the shogun, or military governor) made a concerted effort to round up indigents, prostitutes, and entertainers from the streets and install them in these special quarters in the cities, since regulated, confined entertainers were thought to be preferable to roving itinerants. Throughout the quarters' history as well, large numbers of poor young girls were sold into service there by families who could not support them, and they could not leave the quarters until their considerable debt was repaid.

By the middle of the 1800s, these walled entertainment districts existed in Japan's three largest cities: Yoshiwara in Edo (now Tokyo), Shimmachi in Osaka, and Shimabara in Kyoto. The luxury of the quarters was fueled by the new wealth of the merchants, a class that was on the rise. The pleasure quarters were oases of artistic and sexual license that allowed an escape from the highly regimented Japanese society of the time. The pleasure quarter teahouses where the *yūjo* entertained were like salons frequented by artists, writers, actors, and wrestlers, as well as by men about town and other social strivers.

HOW I LONG FOR THE MAN

WHO CLIMBED MT. YOSHINO

PLUNGING THROUGH THE WHITE SNOW

LYING THICK ON ITS HEIGHTS.

Shizuka (The mistress of Yoshitsune; twelfth century)

RIGHT: *This 1780s print by Shumman shows a summer party at the famous Shikien restaurant on the Sumida river in Edo. Two geisha tune their shamisen in the lower right as the two young male customers, dressed in cool robes of check and plaid, become satiated with food, drink, and women.*

LEFT: *The earliest predecessors to geisha were dancers and musicians who entertained at aristocratic gatherings. Since the most famous was Shizuka, these women came to be called "Shizukas."*

ALLURING ENTERTAINERS OF OLD

LEFT: *Courtesans look out from the balcony of their brothels onto the broad avenue of Yoshiwara, the most famous pleasure quarter of Tokyo. By the time this picture was made in the late nineteenth century, courtesans had lost their predominant cultural status and were selling their charms very cheaply.*

BELOW: *The teahouses were important places in which the courtesans could entertain. Illustrated books recreated these typical teahouse scenes for the growing reading public.*

NO WAY TO SEE HIM

ON THIS MOONLESS NIGHT—

I LIE AWAKE LONGING, BURNING,

BREASTS RACING FIRE

HEART IN FLAMES.

Ono no Komachi (Ninth century)

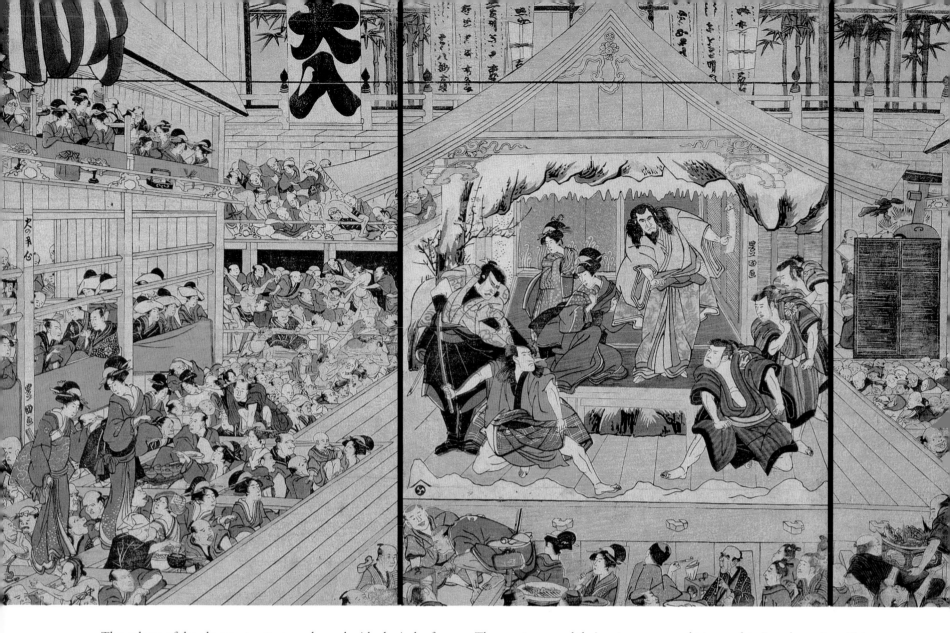

The culture of the pleasure quarters was layered with classical references. The courtesans and their entourages sought to emulate Japan's previous Heian era, the aristocratic golden age from the ninth to twelfth centuries when the beauty and sadness of nature was celebrated in evocative poetry, much of it written by women. The courtesans—and the artists who depicted them—made constant reference to the romantic novel *The Tale of Genji*, written by court figure Lady Murasaki Shikibu in the eleventh century and considered one of the world's greatest novels. The courtesans of the pleasure quarters became adept in all of the most esteemed ancient accomplishments, including calligraphy, poetry, flower arranging, the tea ceremony, dancing, and musicianship.

The world of pleasure that was captured inside the walled entertainment districts was also called "the floating world." In *Tales of the Floating World*, written around 1661, Asai Ryoi described it as:

> Living only for the moment, turning our full attention to the pleasures of the moon, the snow, the cherry blossoms and the maple leaves; singing songs, drinking wine, diverting ourselves in just floating, floating; caring not a whit for the pauperism staring us in the face, refusing to be disheartened, like a gourd floating along with the river current: this is what we call the floating world . . .

The "flower and willow world," another poetic term for the pleasure quarters, was a multi-layered society. A few courtesans were given the highest rank of *tayū* or *oiran* and were treated like royalty, attended by *shinzō* and *kamuro* and various other servants. The *oiran* attempted to compete with each other by showing off their sumptuous luxury in daily parades through the quarters, marching ritualistically in a highly contrived figure-eight step. As time passed, their fashions became more and more elaborate, their robes heavier with quilting and more laden with embroidered gold thread, their hairdos larger and larger with more ornate pins and ornaments. The pitch of rivalry between courtesans over dress and coiffures reached a peak around 1800.

Sophisticated, cultured behavior was expected not only of the courtesans. The privilege of the company of the best courtesans was an expense that few men could afford, and had to be earned by suave manners and wit as well as money. Those who wished to enter the world of pleasure needed guides to smooth the way for them and teach them the correct behavior. There are many humorous stories about the country bumpkin who makes a fool of himself in the pleasure quarters by listening to the wrong advice! Conversely, the ideal romantic story is of the profligate son ruining his family fortune by expending it on his beloved courtesan and then, in despair, committing a love suicide with her. Both of these types of patrons certainly existed. A story that was far more common, and one with a happy ending, was the case of the merchant who paid off the debts of his favorite courtesan in order to marry her.

Only a small percentage of the population had the freedom, resources, or social standing to gain entrance to the pleasure quarters. But those who were denied access could live it vicariously by reading about it in the popular literature. Much of the explosion of literature that was published during this period centered on the goings-on of the world of pleasure. Visual tributes to the actor, wrestler, and courtesan celebrities of the quarters were produced in the form of beautiful hand-colored woodblock prints. Called *ukiyo-e* (prints of the floating world), they were printed with increasingly sophisticated techniques that have yet to be rivaled. Though perhaps poignant for some of its residents, the cultured and mysterious world of the pleasure quarters offered a life of fantasy that inspired poetry in language and image.

> THE MAGNET POINTS TO THE
>
> YOSHIWARA
>
> FROM ANY PLACE WHATEVER.
>
> *An anonymous senryū*
> *(Edo-period satirical poem)*

ABOVE: *Ever since the Edo period, the worlds of courtesans and the Kabuki theater have been closely tied, both in their arts and in their shared projected fantasies. It's easy to spot the courtesans in this depiction of a rowdy audience at a Kabuki play in this late eighteenth-century perspective print by Toyokuni.*

THE GOLDEN AGE OF GEISHA

OPPOSITE: *Two* tatsumi *geisha of the unlicensed Fukugawa quarter share an umbrella as their attendant carries their* shamisen *and lights their way. This late eighteenth-century print by Koryūsai illustrates the special geisha spirit that marked the popular rise of geisha.*

ABOVE: *Two geisha of the early twentieth century, at the ebbing of the golden age of geisha, display their dual arts of dance and* shamisen.

The word *geisha* literally means "arts person," those who hire themselves out for their entertainment skills. Originally they were all male. From the inception of the pleasure quarters, they performed in ways that the high courtesans considered beneath them, as dancers, jesters, drum-beaters, and *shamisen* players. They were thought to be merely a by-product of the pleasure quarters, a peripheral part of the entourage that circled the *oiran* courtesans.

When women geisha began to appear around 1750, they were at first specially designated as *onna geisha* (female geisha). There was much fear that they would compete with the *yūjo* for customers and so there were many restrictions on their behavior. The first female geisha of Yoshiwara was named Kasen. She graduated to the purely entertainment profession after paying off all of her debts. But as time wore on the women came to replace the male geisha, and by about 1800 geisha had become all female.

Geisha originally were allowed to go freely in and out of the pleasure quarters. Later they became as regulated as the *yūjo*; they had to register, and couldn't leave the quarters without special permission. In the quarters, unattractive geisha who presented less of a threat to the *yūjo* were preferred.

From the prologue of a popular puppet play about the pleasure quarters:

THE SUN HAD SET WITH THE

TOLLING OF THE EVENING BELL,

BUT INSIDE THE PLEASURE

QUARTERS MANY LAMPS

WERE LIT,

AND MANY COURTESANS WERE IN

FULL REGALIA.

BELOW: *The first geisha were men. The geisha musicians accompanying the female dancers in this rendering were known as "river-bed folk."*

OPPOSITE: *Westerners frolic in the Gankirō, their own special pleasure house located in Yokohama, in this Yoshikazu print of 1861.*

OPPOSITE: *Geisha rush down Otemma Street where cotton fabrics are sold—perhaps to place an order—in this 1858 Hiroshige print.*

RIGHT: *Okichi of Shimoda was the geisha mistress to Townsend Harris, who came on the Black Ships and was American consul in the late 1850s.*

BELOW LEFT: *Geisha dancers pose to show typical dance gestures, their sleeves tied for easier movement.*

BELOW RIGHT: *A maiko rests in a restaurant by the Kamo river in Kyoto.*

SONG AT DANCE IN JAPAN.

How long will it last?
I do not know his heart.
This morning my thoughts are as
        tangled with anxiety
as my black hair.

Lady Horikawa (Twelfth century)

LAST AUTUMN

THE THREE OF US TOSSED ACORNS

TO THE SCATTERING CARP.

NOW IN THE COLD MORNING

WIND OFF THE POND

HE AND I STAND HAND IN

CHILLING HAND.

Yosano Akiko (1878–1942)

However, geisha, sometimes of uncertain entertainment skills, began to populate unlicensed pleasure quarters. These geisha, particularly, in their independence and verve, took on a new kind of chic known as *iki*. *Yūjo*, the high courtesans of the pleasure quarters, were unfavorably contrasted with the geisha as too stiff, old-fashioned, and overly ornate, and were condemned for their games of duplicitous pretense. Eventually, *yūjo* entirely lost their luster and geisha replaced them, reflecting the new vigor of the nineteenth century when Japan moved into modern times.

The nineteenth century, when geisha life reached its peak, was a time of political ferment. Japan was already ripe for political change when American Admiral Perry and his naval forces succeeded in opening Japan's ports in 1853. The restoration of the emperor then began in earnest; the ensuing battles overthrew the Tokugawa regime that had ruled for more than 250 years. The new nation of Japan began to modernize, industrialize, and even colonize.

Geisha did not just lead fashion, but took on the spirit of heroic revolution. They became involved in the intrigues of the political rebels who were then the founders of the new nation. It is often repeated that the scheme for overthrowing the rulers of the Edo period was hatched in the teahouses of Gion in Kyoto. Several of the national heroes of the new nation married their Gion geisha mistresses and took them to the new capital of Tokyo (formerly Edo) to reign as their wives. Perhaps the fact that former geisha were in governmental circles influenced policy. Changing laws lowered the status of *yūjo* and prostitutes, who were only skilled in the arts of love, and elevated geisha, who were skilled in dance and music.

From the time they first became popular, geisha had long been a favored subject of *ukiyo-e*, the woodblock prints that depicted the "floating world." Now, in this increasingly commercial age, geisha began to figure in postcards and even beer advertisements. They became emblems of modern Japan, providing local color, dancing in the parades, and appearing on tourism posters to attract domestic and foreign visitors alike. The geisha quarters, called *hanamachi*, began to sponsor annual or semi-annual public dances to attract the general public. Geisha, in a little more than one hundred years, had gone from being lively trendsetters to colorful, yet remote, icons.

OPPOSITE: *In this travel poster, two beauties are invigorated by the cool autumn air of Nikko, a tourist spot a few hours from Tokyo, known for its colorful fall foliage.*

ABOVE: *Geisha carried on the tradition of courtesans before them in referring to Genji classics. This Eizan image refers to the 43rd chapter of* **The Tale of Genji.**

29

PREWAR DECADENCE

By the 1920s and 1930s, the same years in which Arthur Golden's character Sayuri comes into her own as a geisha—Japanese modernity had taken a Western turn, and the *iki* of geisha had lost its appeal. The number of geisha was higher than ever before, but other "modern" women were now in the vanguard, described by the new adjective *modan*.

The decades before World War II were a time of decadence. With the influence of Hollywood, magazines, radio programs, popular music and jazz, young men became *mobo* and young Japanese women *moga*, short for modern boy and modern girl. They danced the jitterbug, played tennis, and drank beer and whiskey. Young women considered kimono elegant enough, but too constricting to wear. They cut their long hair into bobs in order to be up-to-date. The range of possible jobs for women in the cities grew—a young lady could now become a store salesclerk, office worker, elevator girl, or, if she was a bit racy, the new rival to the geisha, a *jokyū* or café girl. Like geisha, some of the *jokyū* became celebrities.

Everyone seemed to have an opinion of the geisha's role in contemporary Japan. While some thought they were just an old man's pastime, and modern young men dismissed them as utterly boring, others saw them as important upholders of Japanese tradition. Some geisha, in the hopes of being in vogue once more, began to experiment with the new Western fashions, cutting their hair and getting permanents. There were even experiments with violin playing and revue-style dancing, and gimmicks such as posing semi-nude to draw customers. During this time geisha became much quicker to offer their bodies than they had in the past.

This experimentation was short-lived. The new patriotism of the increasingly militaristic society of the 1930s necessitated a return to traditionalism. This meant a return to favor for the geisha.

OPPOSITE: *In the 1920s and 1930s* jokyū, *or café girls, began to rival geisha in popularity and number. This 1933 painting by Nakamura Gakuryo shows a* jokyū *pausing to observe the lascivious side of the business.*

ABOVE: *A fantasia of colorful Japanese kimono.*

LEFT: *Just as the character of Sayuri was immortalized in paint, so was this* maiko, *seated in a Kyoto garden in this famous 1924 classic by Tsuchida Bakusen.*

ABOVE, BELOW, AND OPPOSITE: *In the decades before the war, many jobs opened up to the young women who were lured by the sophistication of the cities. This series by Nakamura Gakuryo presents some of the attractive possibilities, clockwise from above: an elevator girl, a nurse, a magician, a department store clerk, and a revue girl.*

When I see the moon
Bygone things like floating
clouds return.
Does Autumn come to me alone?

From a geisha song

CHANGES WITH WARTIME

OPPOSITE: *Geisha were the favored entertainers for the military—whether at huge banquets or private affairs for generals.*

ABOVE: *The ideal of an Asian empire led Japan to increasing worldwide warfare. This welcome gate was erected in the flush of victory after wars with China and Russia at the turn of the century.*

 As Japanese aggression in Asia grew during the 1930s, the mood in Japan became increasingly anti-Western. Eastern ideals and Japanese traditions were at first encouraged and then became mandatory. The government blamed the "decadence" of the previous decades on the influence of the West and actively began to curb it. American movies were banned from theaters, and the English language was banned from the schools. Fashion was controlled. Women were no longer allowed to perm their hair. By the 1940s, women were advised to wear *mompe*, or farmer's pants, rather than dresses. An invasion seemed imminent as everyone went through daily military training exercises.

In the midst of these bleak, repressive times, geisha came to be appreciated as emblems of traditional Japan. In the process, the debate over whether geisha should modernize by becoming more westernized was silenced. From this time onward, geisha became the conservators of past traditions. During the war years, military officers replaced prominent industrialists as geishas' patrons. Geisha became leaders in patriotism, as

So it goes

If you're cruel to a woman.

But—

Pamper her,

She puffs with conceit.

You don't suit her fancy,

Her rage can't be beat.

Reprove her, she cries,

And deceive her—before

   your eyes,

Two sprouting horns

Of jealousy arise.

But—

Just knock her off

And she'll haunt you

She will.

A woman is a fearful thing—

Though we can't do

   without them,

Best take care, best take

   care—

A woman is a fearful thing

Korya korya kora

   Geisha song

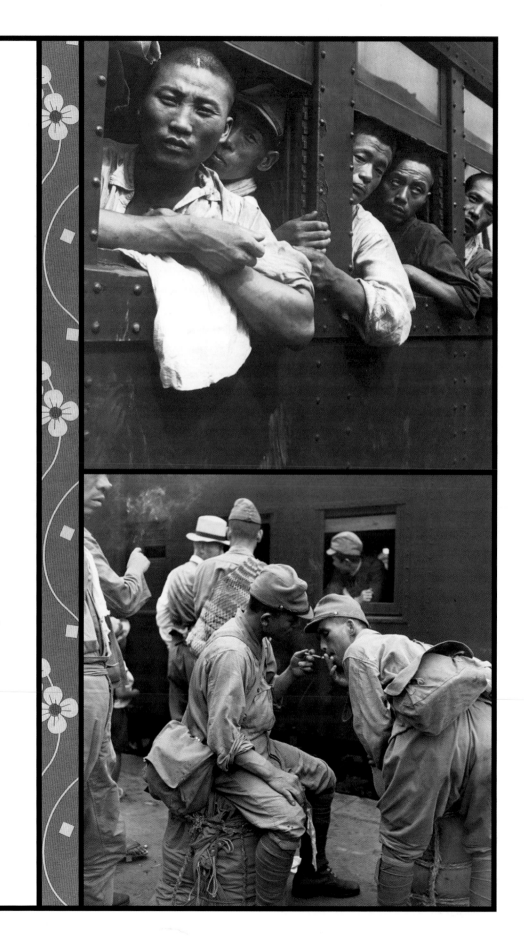

CHANGES WITH WARTIME

CIVIL UNREST UNRELENTING,

AFGHANISTAN, BALUCHISTAN,

    ANNAN, BURMA, INDIA

AND OTHER COUNTLESS SMALL

    COUNTRIES, TOO.

ALL THESE ARE COLONIES OF

    ENGLAND OR OF FRANCE.

IF THIS CONTINUES, THE ORIENT

WILL BE TRAMPLED UNDER

BY THE POWER OF THE WEST.

AND NO COUNTRY WILL RETAIN

ITS PLACE OF EQUALITY.

...ENGLAND, FRANCE,

    GERMANY, RUSSIA—

SHOULD ALL THE ENEMY BE

    STRUCK DOWN

AND THE GLORIOUS FLAG OF THE

    RISING SUN

WAVE O'ER THE HIMALAYAN PEAKS,

WHAT FUN! WHAT JOY!

    —*The Future of Asia*

OPPOSITE, TOP AND BOTTOM: *Virtually all able-bodied Japanese men were conscripted to fight for the Empire of the Rising Sun during what was later called in Japan "the fifteen years war."*

BELOW: *This cover to an envelope of geisha postcards says, "these beauties are cheering our imperial army," showing the popular approval of the alliance between geisha and the military.*

皇軍御慰問

京美人絵はがき

LONGING,
   LONGING
TO BE TOGETHER
I FRET MY
   DAYS AWAY.
EVER SO ONCE
   IN A WHILE
WE STEAL A NIGHT
   TOGETHER,
   AND PART
LONGING,
   LONGING.

PARTING IS
   MERELY
   LONGING,
   NEVER
FAREWELL—
THE TEMPLE BELL
   SOUNDING
   AT DAWN.

*Anonymous ko-uta
(geisha song)*

they entertained at parties for the military and saw the officers off to battle. In *Memoirs of a Geisha*, Sayuri's liaison with General Tottori Junnosuke is typical of the times. This type of "insider status" meant that when it became hard for ordinary civilians to get basic food and supplies, geisha could usually get what they needed.

It was not until the very end of the war in 1944 that all teahouses and geisha houses were closed. Geisha joined much of the rest of the non-military populace and were conscripted to work in factories to produce the machinery of war. Many geisha, like Sayuri, used their connections to pull strings so as to get comparatively easy work.

CHANGES WITH WARTIME

After the Japanese surrender in August 1945, the government opened up all of the establishments that had been closed in 1944. A new organization of establishment owners formed a league called the Recreation and Amusement Association to recruit women. Although they needed at least 5,000 women, only 1,360 responded to the advertisements.

In January 1946, General MacArthur's headquarters ordered the abolishment of legalized prostitution. The result was "red-line zones," areas where American servicemen were prohibited to enter, but which were open to Japanese for freelance prostitution. Finally, on May 12, 1956, all prostitution in Japan was declared illegal. Geisha simply tightened their *obis*, adjusted themselves to new times and policies, formed new associations, and survived.

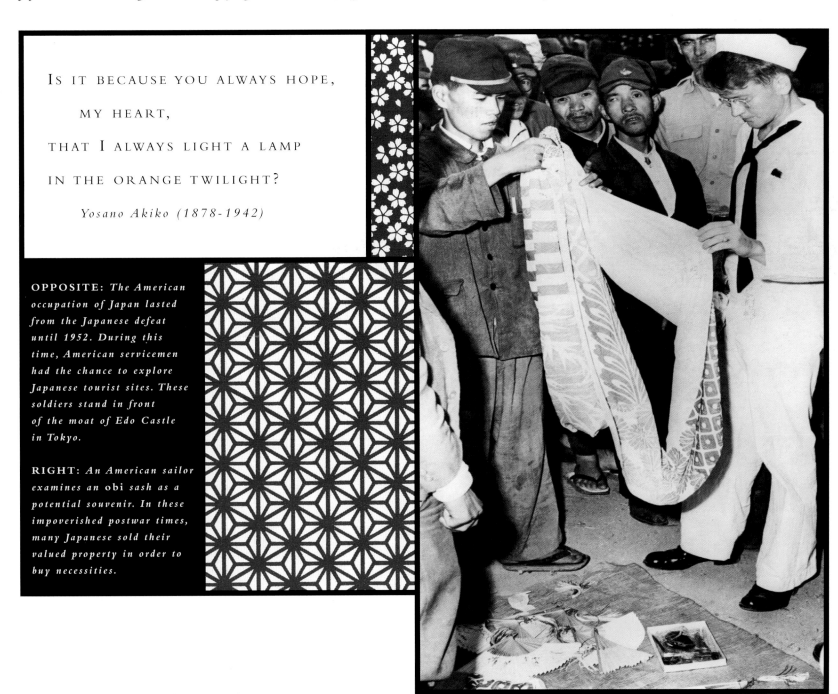

Is it because you always hope,

my heart,

that I always light a lamp

in the orange twilight?

Yosano Akiko (1878-1942)

OPPOSITE: *The American occupation of Japan lasted from the Japanese defeat until 1952. During this time, American servicemen had the chance to explore Japanese tourist sites. These soldiers stand in front of the moat of Edo Castle in Tokyo.*

RIGHT: *An American sailor examines an obi sash as a potential souvenir. In these impoverished postwar times, many Japanese sold their valued property in order to buy necessities.*

THE LIFE
OF A GEISHA

A geisha cannot survive without maintaining a strong web of relationships among the members of her community. Whether these relationships are positive or negative, they support a geisha in her individual niche. A geisha's use of familial names for those most important to her shows the family-type of support that is necessary. The success as a geisha of the character Sayuri was not only due to her beauty or talent, but also to the support of her "elder sister," Mameha.

In the course of their careers, there were certain rites of passage common to all geisha trained before the war. Geisha inherited this life course from the *yūjo* courtesans before them.

A geisha usually was sold to an establishment as a young girl when her family could not support her. She started out as a *shikomi*, an indentured servant who did menial tasks. Her house was run by a person called *okāsan* (mother), usually a retired geisha. The *shikomi* had to

OPPOSITE: *The okāsan (mother figure) straightens the kimono layers of an elaborately-dressed young woman with an old-fashioned oiran look.*

ABOVE: Maiko *show off the vibrant design and color of their long obi sashes as they gaze across the river in Kyoto.*

IN THE RIGHT OF NOW,

SUCH THINGS YOU SAY!

TWO BUTTERFLIES TIED

BY IMPOSSIBLE DREAMS.

YET WE FLUTTER ALONG TO

THE END OF THE END.

An anonymous Ko-uta (geisha song)

pay particular attention to the needs of the full geisha who earned the money of the house. If the girl showed signs of talent, she would start lessons in dance and music at a local geisha school, starting at about age seven. After spending half the day at school, in the remaining time she had to practice for hours and be sure to complete her domestic tasks as well.

As a teenager, when she was deemed ready, she became an apprentice geisha, called *maiko* in Kyoto and *hangyoku* or *oshaku* in Tokyo. She was dressed in a bright kimono with long *furisode* sleeves. She began to wear her hair in the "split-peach" style in which the hair in her chignon is split to reveal a small triangle of fabric. In order to be an apprentice, she had to have an *onē san* (elder sister) who was willing to take her to her appointments so that she could learn from *minarai* (observing). The apprentice and geisha went through a sisterhood ceremony similar to a wedding, exchanging three sips out of a cup of sake three times. This was called the *san san kudo*.

A geisha would go to the highest bidder for her *mizuage*, her loss of virginity and launching into full womanhood. A ceremony of sake sipping would again take place. As a marker of this significant change in her life, red fabric was placed in her "split-peach" hairstyle. Like the changes in a woman's dress that occurred after a typical Japanese marriage, this made the geisha's transition evident for all to see.

LEFT: *All the geisha, apprentices, and servants of one house line up for this photograph taken in the late nineteenth century.*

ABOVE: *Geisha dressed in kimono decorated with calligraphy wait for their turn to dance at a festival.*

RIGHT: *A geisha dresses up like her predecessor, the oiran, with multiple hairsticks, high slippers, and her obi sash down her front.*

BELOW: *Maiko musicians playing the drums and flute pose with two dancers.*

When a geisha reached full status, she would *erikae o suru* (turn her collar). This meant she would turn back part of the white color of the under-kimono to reveal a small portion of red underclothes beneath. She wore it this way for the ceremonies in which she was introduced. At this point she changed her kimono to the more simply patterned short-sleeved style of a mature woman.

Reaching fully independent status as a geisha almost invariably involved getting a steady patron, or *danna*. He would provide her with financial support, sometimes enough to establish her own house.

The most decisive break of a geisha's career was to marry. They also might leave the *hanamachi* to become someone's full-time mistress. Many geisha, however, stayed on in the quarters to reign as *okāsan* and manage their own house of geisha. There were many geisha who, after a bad marriage or a broken affair, would return to their former lives in which they felt most comfortable.

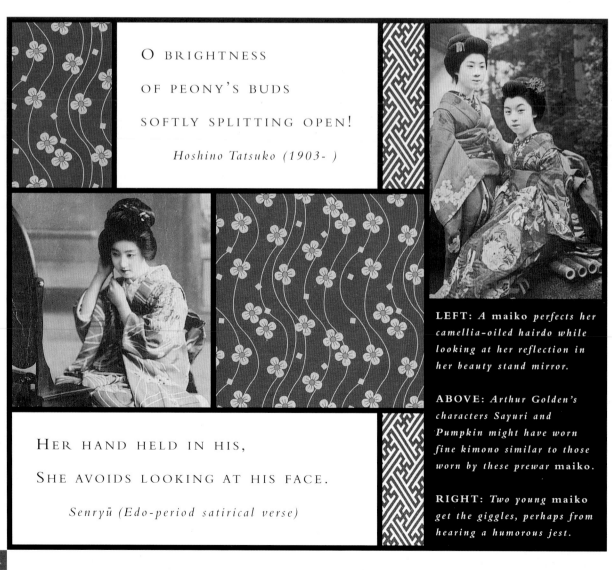

O BRIGHTNESS
OF PEONY'S BUDS
SOFTLY SPLITTING OPEN!

Hoshino Tatsuko (1903-)

HER HAND HELD IN HIS,
SHE AVOIDS LOOKING AT HIS FACE.

Senryū (Edo-period satirical verse)

LEFT: *A* maiko *perfects her camellia-oiled hairdo while looking at her reflection in her beauty stand mirror.*

ABOVE: *Arthur Golden's characters Sayuri and Pumpkin might have worn fine kimono similar to those worn by these prewar* maiko.

RIGHT: *Two young* maiko *get the giggles, perhaps from hearing a humorous jest.*

江戸八景
本妙寺
暮雲

THE CHARMS OF A GEISHA

The idea of "charm" can differ among various cultures and times. Indeed, an American visitor fortunate enough to visit a party in the Gion geisha district of Kyoto where geisha are present might be disappointed. It is often remarked that geisha are too artificial: Their white facial powder is too thick, their tittering laughter is irritating, and their movements are strange. Their singing might seem wailful, and the accompanying *shamisen* music twanging without a melody. The dancing, which is done to a very different sense of rhythm than in Western music, can seem incomprehensible. Distant in time from the culture in which geisha emerged, many Japanese of the younger generation do not appreciate geisha, either. They might not find geisha's movements and melodies unfamiliar, but they would likely think them just too

OPPOSITE: *In this Kunisada print, a nineteenth-century geisha shows the height of* iki *sensibility, lifting her relatively simply designed kimono while jumping to shore from her boat, and baring her foot to the snowy elements.*

ABOVE: *A modern-day* maiko *pauses on a Gion lane, lifting the skirt of her bright yellow kimono with her left hand, as is traditional.*

old-fashioned. To the foreigner with an open mind or to the Japanese with a taste for the past, however, the atmosphere of a geisha party combines color, harmony, sound, and movement with intelligence and humor. The culminating sensibility radiates a rare sense of social intimacy.

The charm of geisha balances unaffected sincerity with highly developed artfulness. It goes without saying that geisha must possess a certain sensuality. The word for this in Japanese is *iroke*, or literally "the spirit of color." This is not simply sex appeal, but a sense of style created by the aesthetic effect of the clothing and body language. It is very evident in the give-and-take of conversation. It also depends on the timing and timbre of the laughter and on an almost cloying attentiveness combined with light teasing.

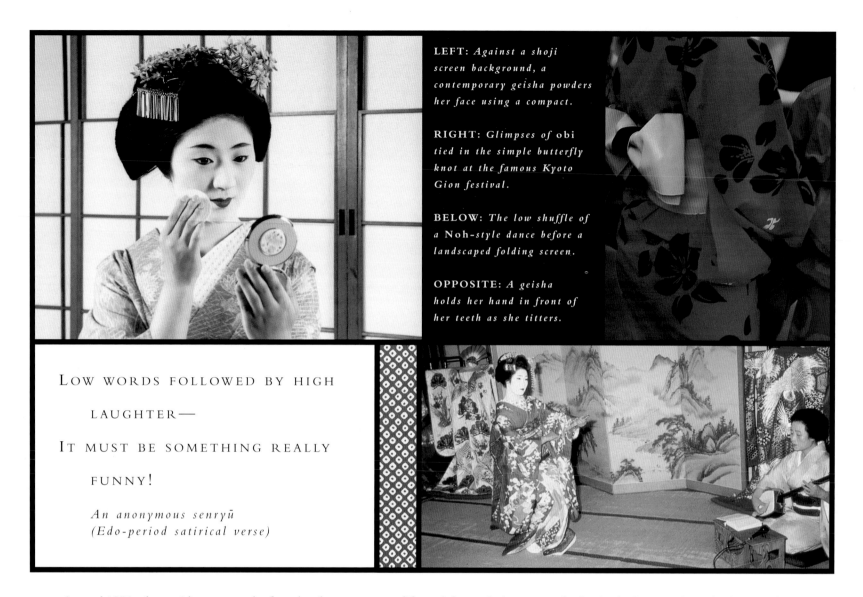

LEFT: *Against a shoji screen background, a contemporary geisha powders her face using a compact.*

RIGHT: *Glimpses of obi tied in the simple butterfly knot at the famous Kyoto Gion festival.*

BELOW: *The low shuffle of a Noh-style dance before a landscaped folding screen.*

OPPOSITE: *A geisha holds her hand in front of her teeth as she titters.*

LOW WORDS FOLLOWED BY HIGH LAUGHTER—

IT MUST BE SOMETHING REALLY FUNNY!

*An anonymous senryū
(Edo-period satirical verse)*

Around 1800 when geisha came to the fore, they began to exemplify a subtle, yet daring, sense of style. Geisha became the embodiment of *iki*, a word still used today to describe a certain cool, chic attitude. It was a casual elegance, the power of understatement, of knowing how not to be overdone. One hundred and fifty years ago a geisha wore light make-up, a kimono of solid colors or a simple pattern, with the *obi* tied plainly in the back. The geisha's simple look was partially the result of regulations meant to prevent geisha from rivaling *yūjo*—but this backfired. The geisha's look, the very antithesis of the *yūjo's*, made the *yūjo* seem old-fashioned. Geisha had just a few hair pins whereas *yūjo* could look like a many-legged insect. A *yūjo's* heavily padded robes done up in silver and gold thread with dragons climbing up the skirts or embellished everywhere with puffy chrysanthemums were too restrictive for the independent-spirited geisha. The geisha replaced *yūjo* by embodying the defiant spirit that reflected the revolutionary changes of the times.

Iki was chic born of some adversity. *Iki* came from the particular type of courage that geisha had—to live independently, for their art alone. For instance, as a sign of their strength of character, geisha never wore *tabi* socks. *Ukiyo-e* prints often show a geisha's bare toes set off against jet-black lacquered clogs, poking defiantly and provocatively out of a kimono. It is all the more *iki* when the bare-toed geisha is walking through snow. The geisha could also affect a slight masculinity. Some of the swagger and brash bravura of the city of Edo (now Tokyo) was part of the attitude where *iki* emerged. In Edo's Fukugawa, geisha began the fashion of dressing in *haori*, originally men's jackets, taking on an androgynous sensuality with a practicality that caused it to be gradually adopted by all women in kimono.

Today, geisha are no longer the trendsetters of style. They are upholders of tradition, dressing in kimono on a daily basis unlike very few other Japanese women. For formal occasions, they have taken on the look of the *yūjo* who died out: wearing heavy make-up and weighty, ornate kimonos. But geisha still are fashionable, if within a smaller niche. Dress is a part of their art. The taste evident in a geisha's dress and the perfection of her hairdo is the outward indication of the level of her aesthetic sensibilities. Geisha still spend most of their income on their appearance, going into debt to buy new luxurious *obi* sashes and elegant kimonos in the most recent styles. If she can display the work of the most artistic of kimono dyers, then all the better for her reputation. A geisha seeks to dazzle her guests with the pure artistry of her kimono, as framed by the shoji door of the room. Although geisha no longer impact fashion in general, they do still generate new styles in kimono—in the 1970s geisha were the first to start the fashion for pastel kimonos.

It may seem puzzling to Westerners that a geisha's charm is supposed to increase with age. There are said to be two types of geisha. There are the young pretty ones, who dazzle with their beauty and innocence and soon find someone to marry. They retire with hardly a ripple. The other type depends less on her good looks than her wit of conversation. She captivates her guests with her repartee. She knows the power of a good anecdote and the art of teasing without offending. Beneath her quick laugh and bright sense of humor she has an insight into people and an acceptance of the foibles of humanity. This type of geisha is likely to reign in her *hanamachi* into old age, and be much missed after her death.

PUNISHED IN THE MOMENT
OF LOVE
I LOOKED BACK
AND SAW THE JEALOUSY OF
THE GODS
OVERFLOW THE MILKY WAY

Baba Akiko (1928-)

THE ARTS OF A GEISHA

OPPOSITE: *Fandancer, Country Maiden Autumn Dancer, and the Courtesan Full Moon Blossom—dancers from the Nikawa festival, impromptu theater that was performed in the Yoshiwara pleasure quarters, by Utamaro.*

ABOVE: *Geisha provide the rhythm of the dance with drum and flute.*

A geisha's personal pride as well as her standing among her peers is dependent on her *gei*, or arts. The *gei* have been important to a geisha since the profession's beginnings, when the geisha were hired for their skills in singing and dance. It is the same today, when the young women who become geisha do so largely because of their love of traditional music and dance. As geisha they can perform as professionals rather than pay to perform as amateurs.

The *gei* of geisha is primarily comprised of *shamisen* playing and traditional dancing, but it also encompasses any number of other traditional arts: calligraphy, the ability to compose poetry, and the tea ceremony, for example. Prewar geisha, who underwent many years of hard training, were versatile in many styles of both music and dance. Geisha today are most often conversant in just one style of either music or dance.

Geisha must attain technical precision in order for their art to become second nature. They first learn to play by rote. Learning by rote is important so that a geisha can then adapt to the moment and adjust her playing to complement the singer or dancer. The more spontaneous the occasion, the greater the geisha's true artistry. Rigorous practice techniques from an early age used to be the rule—Chiyo's practicing outside in the dead of winter was typical. The hardship was thought to ensure that the voice would sing and fingers would be nimble in any tough condition.

GEISHA AND KABUKI

There is a strong link between the geisha's arts and Kabuki, a form of Japanese theater in which singing, dancing, and spectacular staging are combined with stylized acting. The entertainer Okuni, a young Shinto priestess, first performed Kabuki dances and comic sketches around 1600. The display of the charms of her troupe on the stage (and availability of them offstage), caused public disturbances, and in 1629 women were abolished from the stage. Thereafter, Kabuki became entirely male—even in female roles—evolving into the popular traditional theater that is still performed today.

In addition to the historical connection between the feminine allure of Kabuki performer Okuni and the later female entertainers known as geisha, there is also an artistic link. Both male Kabuki performers and geisha mingled within the confines of the pleasure quarters, where (privately) female dancing was still allowed after 1629. Thus, the *gei* of the geisha came to borrow directly from the repertoire of Kabuki. Geisha dancing, especially that of the Tokyo school, relies heavily on Kabuki dance styles, while geisha songs are often the same ones played on the Kabuki stage.

THE SHAMISEN

The *shamisen* is an instrument consisting of a drum made of catskin with three strings of braided silk extending outward along a long neck of

WAITING ANXIOUSLY FOR YOU,
UNABLE TO SLEEP, BUT FALLING
 INTO A DOZE—
ARE THOSE WORDS OF LOVE
FLOATING TO MY PILLOW,
OR IS THIS TOO A DREAM....
MY EYES OPEN AND HERE IS MY
 TEAR-DRENCHED SLEEVE.
PERHAPS IT WAS A SUDDEN RAIN.

An anonymous ko-uta (geisha song)

OPPOSITE: *In this nineteenth-century ukiyo-e painting, the male customer in his striped kimono is drawn by the charms of the lady to his right tuning her shamisen.*

ABOVE: *Kabuki actors enact a struggle with puppets in a dance.*

LEFT: *Geisha, always great fans of Kabuki, look over the actor list.*

THE ARTS OF A GEISHA

redwood, with three ivory pegs for tuning. It is played with an ivory "plectrum" (pick). Its music is designed to accompany the human voice. Played well, it has great emotional resonance.

Geisha came into vogue along with the demand for *shamisen* music. Beginning in the 1700s, geisha were hired to play the latest tunes on this plaintive-sounding instrument that had been imported from China via Korea. If there is any one thing that symbolizes the geisha, it is this banjo-like instrument. To the geisha musician, a *shamisen* is her dearest friend. She may call it affectionately her "o-shami." In *ukiyo-e* prints, the presence of a *shamisen* invariably identifies a geisha more surely than does hairstyle or dress. Today, not all geisha perform with the *shamisen* publicly, but all are trained to play it.

THE ARTS OF A GEISHA

三味線も廓も
ひさぐく
三味線
彩好の春
くうきくろ
つり
松樹園在雲人
とろき居まゐひて
をそしを三味線も
きうく
城塔山
船迤屋綱人

（vertical Japanese calligraphy）

I REMEMBER THE DAYS
WHEN THE LILY
BRILLIANT WHITE
WAS QUEEN OF THE SUMMER
FIELDS.

Yosano Akiko (1878-1942)

OPPOSITE: *Perhaps on her way to perform at a party, a geisha, her shamisen behind her, leans back with a distant thought, not feeling the coldness of the weather.*

ABOVE LEFT: *As a geisha plays, the revellers at the party grow wilder by the minute.*

ABOVE CENTER: *For centuries in Japan, outdoor tea stands have provided a pleasant place to flirt.*

ABOVE RIGHT: *A tea cup and ladle on a stand make a pretty sight.*

Originally, the *shamisen* was used to accompany folk melodies. Out of this grew the tradition of *ko-uta* (short songs) and *naga-uta* (long songs). There are different types of songs in the repertoire today. There are the romantic songs that read like poetry. Often they use natural imagery. Many are about waiting for one's lover. In contrast, there are tunes called *kappore*, sometimes folk tunes from the provinces, merry tunes that get everyone to pick up their heels. These are more dependent on the rhythmic sound of the words than poetic imagery.

DANCE

Today, the most successful geisha are primarily dancers and are mainly seen by the public in dance performances. Geisha are not the only performers of traditional Japanese dance styles, but they are a large part of the reason it has been kept alive. The dances can range from highly choreographed performances in seasonal galas to country geisha dancing in a parade on a local festival day.

Though the movements of traditional dance may seem deceptively simple to a Westerner, they are not made simply to the beat as ballroom dancing or ballet. The body's center of balance is quite low; the feet sometimes slide bent-kneed along the floor; there can be a flash of action after what may seem like almost no movement.

The kimono is part of the reason for the uniquely Japanese dance movements. The *obi* sash keeps the torso relatively rigid, and the skirt of the kimono keeps the legs from stepping very wide. The length and weight of the sleeves predispose the arms to maneuver around a certain circumference.

Today, there are many schools of traditional dance. The geisha of Gion practice a classical style influenced by the measured, stately movements of the *Noh* theater. It is very slow, somber and tied to ancient stories. It consists of very formalized gestures in which the play of the fan is used as a prop to indicate many things. Its characteristic movement is the slow sliding of the feet along the floor without lifting the heels. The schools of dance in other districts are related to the livelier and more colorful Kabuki style of dance. It includes dramatic stamping that is sometimes punctuated by leaps and bounds. Though the speed of movement differs between the Kyoto and Tokyo schools, movements in both are highly controlled. Dances of the countryside are performed on the street for festival days or during a party to lighten spirits. These consist of simple movements to an easy beat so that anyone can join in, and have a lot more freedom of movement. To prevent the kimono from constricting the arms and legs, the skirts and sleeves are pulled up.

The public performance of geisha dances go back more than a hundred years. The Gion quarters started their Miyako dances in 1872, the Osaka geisha followed in 1882, and Tokyo began in 1925. Aside from a short break during the war, the annual spring and autumn performances have been continuous. There is a friendly rivalry between the geisha quarters in these shows. Scores of dancers practice for months to try to give the performance of a lifetime. Geisha help to create the group of twenty or more musicians and singers necessary for the performance. For the judges (comprised of other geisha and Kabuki actors), the dancers strive to attain the purest artistry, while for the public, they make sure to provide an incredible spectacle. In quality of choreography and production, costume and make-up, these performances rival Kabuki theater. Through these performances, the arts of the geisha are sure to endure, perhaps for another hundred years to come.

THE OBJECT OF LOVE,

THE OBJECT OF HATRED.

*An anonymous senryū
(Edo-period satirical verse)*

OPPOSITE: *Geisha—among Japan's foremost traditional dancers—practice the subtleties of the dancer's art for decades in order to achieve greatness.*

BELOW: *Ready to be judged by their peers and appreciated by their fans, geisha perform in the gala spring performance.*

A F T E R W O R D :
G E I S H A   T O D A Y

Periodically, articles in the Japanese media make geisha sound like an endangered species. They usu-

ally focus on how there are now only a handful of *maiko*, or geisha in training, in Kyoto and that

these are young ladies recruited from the provinces who have agreed to be *maiko* for only a few years. Perhaps

in the next few decades geisha will die out. However, as scarce in number as geisha have become, as long as

geisha keep Japanese traditional dance and music alive they will be treasured, and will most likely persist as cherished emblems of Japan.

The life of a geisha has changed since prewar days. Girls are no longer sold to geisha houses. *Mizuage* is a thing of the past. Though many

geisha still have patrons for practical economic reasons, a geisha is free to choose her patron and even to have other boyfriends. These days, a

young woman is most likely to want to become a geisha for her devotion to dance or to the *shamisen*. Her training can be as short as a year,

ABOVE: *Perhaps just returning from an excursion in the countryside, a* maiko *walks the Kyoto platform of the* shinkansen *(bullet train), the symbol of Japanese modernity.*

although she will likely study one of the arts for much longer. Whereas more than a century ago geisha were at the vanguard of chic and were emulated celebrities, they now work in a more sheltered world to uphold tradition. If it is money she is after, a young woman would be better off becoming a hostess at a hostess club than a geisha. Evening gatherings at hostess clubs function in much the same way as geisha parties did in the past. High-class hostesses are beautiful, sumptuously dressed, witty women who wear the latest fashions. The clubs, especially in Akasaka or Ginza, are places where the genial atmosphere smoothes the way for the resolution of business agreements that were too tricky for negotiations at the office. These days, an important man's mistress is more likely to be an ex-hostess than an ex-geisha. Hostesses, much more than geisha, are now likely to be the brokers of business and government secrets. The best hostesses can, like geisha before them, reign at conversation or know when to keep silent. By middle age, hostesses can become financially independent by becoming *mama-san* of their own clubs.

The role of geisha has also diminished in recent decades as the nature of socializing and sexuality has changed. The Japanese sexual revolution has evolved through many generations. Before the war, there were the café girls. After the war, *sutorippu* (strips) were all the rage. "Love Hotels" that rent by the hour started to be popular in the 1960s. *Furin*, the "immoral love" of housewives who wanted to have a little fling for excitement, or merely add a little bit to their shopping budget, was the excitement of the 1980s. The most recent sexual freedom has school girls with portable phones taking advantage of the "telephone clubs," wherein they rendezvous with male callers for money in order to buy status objects like brand-name handbags. Many of these trends are more of a media topic than generally prevalent, but all point to drastic changes in the sexual morés of Japan.

In the Japan of today, it is perhaps unsurprising that the erotic allure of those accomplished in the arts forged a few hundred years ago has diminished. But geisha still serve a purpose in Japan. The most lavish parties of the largest firms still use geisha entertainment. In the future, as long as there are young women who want to perform traditional dance and *shamisen* professionally, there probably will be geisha. And geisha will remain as long as there are Japanese men desiring to participate in the world that only geisha can create—whether just to show off their refinement and sophistication, or because they truly treasure the poetry of the past.

THE FIREFLIES' LIGHT
HOW EASILY IT GOES ON
HOW EASILY IT GOES OUT AGAIN.

Chine-Jo (Late seventeenth century)

RIGHT: *Modern conveniences and transportation help keep this geisha on schedule as she checks on her next appointment.*

GLOSSARY

danna The patron of a geisha; the same word used for husband or keeper of a shop.

erikae o suru The turning of the collar that marks the transition from apprentice to full geisha.

furisode The long "swinging sleeves" of a kimono worn by younger, unmarried women. Distinguishes apprentice geisha from full geisha.

gei "Arts"; skills.

geisha Person who is skilled in the arts.

hanamachi Geisha quarters.

hangyoku Apprentice geisha in Tokyo. *Oshaku* is also used.

haori A jacket worn over kimono. Originally male attire, it became women's wear after geisha began wearing it.

ikebana The art of flower arrangement.

iki The nineteenth-century concept of cool chic that geisha embodied.

iroke Sex appeal; glamour.

jokyū The café girls who began to rival geisha in the 1920s; predecessors to bar hostesses.

Kabuki The lively popular theater that originated in the seventeenth century.

kamuro A child attendant of a courtesan (*yūjo*).

karyūkai The "flower and willow world," a poetic term for geisha society.

ko-uta "Short songs" for voice and shamisen.

maiko Apprentice geisha in Kyoto.

mama-san What the female manager/owner of a hostess club is called.

minarai To learn from observation.

mizuage Deflowering of an apprentice geisha.

mobo/moga Short for modern boy, modern girl. Slightly derogatory terms used in the 1920s and 1930s for westernized Japanese youth.

momoware "Split peach" hairstyle traditionally worn by young girls, now worn by only Kyoto *maiko*.

naga-uta "Long songs" for voice and *shamisen*.

Noh The usually slow and stately school of theater and dance that originated in the fourteenth century.

obi The long sash used to tie the kimono.

oiran A general term for high-ranking courtesans, used in the latter part of the Edo period. The term replaced *tayū*.

okāsan "Mother," the owner/manager of a geisha establishment.

onēsan "Older sister," a geisha who takes an apprentice geisha under her wing to teach her the tricks of the trade.

saburuko "Ones who serve," the original prostitutes in Japan.

san san kudo Three sips of sake three times; the ceremony for the marriage bond. In the geisha world, performed when an apprentice is sponsored by an *onēsan*, and when a geisha gets a *danna*.

senryū Satirical verse that was popular in the latter half of the Edo period.

shamisen A three-stringed banjo-like instrument (sometimes spelled *samisen*).

shikomi An indentured servant of a geisha establishment who did menial tasks before becoming an apprentice geisha (now obsolete).

shinkansen The "Bullet Train"; super-speed trains launched in 1964 in conjunction with the Tokyo Olympics.

shinzō Attendants of high-ranking courtesans.

shirabyōshi Dancers/courtesans from the tenth to sixteenth centuries.

Shizuka The name of the most famous *shirabyōshi* who became the mistress of the great hero Yoshitsune. Her name later became a term for women like her.

tatsumi geisha Another word for geisha of the unlicensed brothel district of Fukugawa. Fukugawa was in the southeast, or *tatsumi* section of Edo.

tayū High-ranking courtesans during the first part of the Edo period.

ukiyo The "floating world," a poetic term for the world of entertainment in the Edo period.

ukiyo-e "Pictures of the floating world"; the popular woodblock prints that arose and became highly sophisticated during the Edo period; can refer to paintings as well.

yūjo "Play-women;" courtesans of all ranks during the Edo period.

yūkaku The pleasure quarters.

EARLY MODERN
AND MODERN
JAPANESE PERIODS

Edo (Tokugawa) period
1615–1868

Meiji period
1868–1911

Taishō period
1912–1925

Shōwa period
1926–1988

SELECTED BIBLIOGRAPHY

Cobb, Jodi. *Geisha: The Life, the Voices, the Art.* New York: Alfred A. Knopf, 1997.

Crihfield, Liza. *Ko-uta: Little Songs of the Geisha World.* Tokyo: Charles A. Tuttle, 1979.

Dalby, Liza Crihfield. *Geisha.* Berkeley: University of California Press, 1983.

De Becker, J.E. *The Nightless City or the History of the Yoshiwara Yukwaku.* Tokyo: Charles A. Tuttle, 1960.

Golden, Arthur. *Memoirs of a Geisha.* New York: Alfred A. Knopf, Inc., 1997.

Hibbett, Howard. *The Floating World in Japanese Literature.* Tokyo: Charles A. Tuttle, 1959.

Jenkins, Donald. *The Floating World Revisited.* (exhibition catalog) Portland Art Museum and University of Hawaii Press, 1993.

Kobayashi, Tadashi. *Edo Beauties in Ukiyo-e: The James A. Michener Collection.* (exhibition catalog) Honolulu Academy of Arts, 1994.

Lillehoj, Elizabeth. *Woman in the Eyes of Man: Images of Women in Japanese Art from the Field Museum.* (exhibition catalog) The Field Museum, 1995.

Nagai Kafu. *Geisha in Rivalry [Ude kurabe].* Translated by Kurt Meissner. Tokyo: Charles A. Tuttle, 1963.

Scott, A. C. *The Flower and Willow World.* London: Heinemann, 1959.

Seigle, Celia Segawa. *Yoshiwara: The Glittering World of the Japanese Courtesan.* Honolulu: University of Hawaii Press, 1993.

Swinton, Elizabeth de Sabato. *The Women of the Pleasure Quarter.* (exhibition catalog) Hudson Hills Press, 1995.

Yamata, Kikou. *Three Geishas.* Translated by Emma Craufurd. London: Cassell & Co. Ltd., 1956.

CREDITS

TEXT CREDITS

Page 10: Holme, C.G. *Glimpses of Old Japan from Japanese Colour Prints: The Geisha.* London: The Studio Publications, p. 8. **Page 11:** Translated by Crihfield, Liza. *Ko-uta: Little Songs of the Geisha World.* Toyko: Charles A. Tuttle, 1979, p. 67. **Page 12:** Translated by Jane Hirshfield with Mariko Aratani in Hirshfield, Jane with Mariko Aratani, *The Ink Dark Moon: Love Poems* by Ono no Komachi and Izumi Shikibu, *Women of the Ancient Court of Japan.* New York: Vintage Books, 1986, p. 14. **Page 13:** Translated by R.H. Blyth in Blyth, R.H. *Edo Satirical Verse Anthologies.* Tokyo: The Hokuseido Press, 1961, p. 292. **Page 16:** Translated by Kenneth Rexroth and Ikuko Atsumi in Rexroth, Kenneth and Ikuko Atsumi. *Women Poets of Japan.* New York: New Directions Publishing Corporation, 1977, p. 40. **Page 19:** Hirshfeld, p. 6. **Page 21:** Blyth, p. 138. **Page 24:** Adapted from Scott, A.C. *The Flower and Willow World: A Study of the Geisha.* London: Heinemann, 1959, p. 41. **Page 27:** Rexroth, p. 41. **Page 29:** Rexroth, p. 63. **Page 33:** Scott, p. 197. **Page 36:** Adapted from Crihfield, p 95. **Page 37:** "The Future of Asia" translated by Carol Gluck in Gluck, Carol. *Japan's Modern Myths: Ideology in the Late Meiji Period.* Princeton, NJ: Princeton University Press, 1985, p. 131-132. **Page 38:** Crihfield, p. 77. **Page 39:** Rexroth, p. 65. **Page 42:** Crihfield, p. 40. **Page 44:** Top: Rexroth, p. 83; Bottom: Blyth, p. 28. **Page 48:** Blyth, p. 17. **Page 49:** Rexroth, p. 75. **Page 52:** Crihfield, p. 32. **Page 55:** Rexroth, p. 64. **Page 57:** Blyth, p. 85. **Page 59:** Rexroth, p. 52.

PHOTO CREDITS

Half title page: Vintage postcard from Davis Vintage Collectibles, 110 West 25th Street #307, New York, NY 10001, http://www.nypen.com **Title page:** *A Geisha and Her Servant* by Kitao Shigemasa (1739-1820) c.1777, woodblock print. Honolulu Academy of Arts, Gift of James A. Michener, 1991 (21,756). **Dedication page:** Plate IV by Hokkei from Holme, C.G. *Glimpses of Old Japan from Japanese Colour Prints: The Geisha*. London: The Studio Limited. **Page 6:** *Maiko rinsen* by Tsuchida Bakusen, 1924. From the collection of The National Museum of Modern Art, Tokyo. **Page 7:** Upper left: © CORBIS/ Asian Art & Archaeology by Yoshitoshi; Upper right: Vintage postcard envelope. Bottom: Vintage postcards from Davis Vintage Collectibles. **Page 8:** Vintage postcard from Davis Vintage Collectibles. **Page 10:** *Mt. Fuji on Fine Day* by Hokusai Katsushika (1760-1849). Series: *The 36 Views of Mt. Fuji, Ukiyo-e*. **Page 11:** Vintage postcards from Davis Vintage Collectibles. **Page 12:** Top right: FPG International; Bottom left and middle: vintage postcards; Bottom right: *Mt. Fuji from Misakagoe Pass* by Ando Hiroshige (1797-1858). Series: *The 36 Views of Mt. Fuji, Ukiyo-e*. **Page 13:** Vintage postcards from Davis Vintage Collectibles; Bottom right: *Kyoto Meisho* by Ando Hiroshige (1797-1858). **Page 14:** *Ukifune* (*A Boat upon the Waters*), from Genji Monogatari (*The Tale of Genji*), woodblock print from the series *Tosa Meika Gafu* (*Famous Illustrations by the Tosa School*), 1896 by Mitsunoki. The Field Museum, Chicago, IL (Boone Collection) A112739_2c. Photograph by John Weinstein. **Page 15:** © CORBIS/

Asian Art & Archaeology by Yoshitoshi. **Page 16:** *Two Shizukas* © Art Institute of Chicago/W. Gookin/Archive Photos. **Page 17:** *The Shikian Restaurant* (circa 1787-1788) woodblock print by Kubo Shumman (1757-1820) Copyright © The British Museum, ref. 1924/3-27.09. **Page 18:** Yoshiwara, Tokyo photograph circa 1900 from Rainbow Creations, P.O. Box 8935, Universal City, CA 91618, http://www.19cphoto.com **Page 19:** Line drawings circa 1800s from The Kimono House, Inc., 93 East 7th Street, New York, NY 10009. **Page 20-21:** *Inside a Kabuki Theater* (late eighteenth century) woodblock print by Utagawa Toyokuni (1769-1825) Copyright © The British Museum, ref.1907/ S-31.491. **Page 22:** *Night Rain at Nakacho* by Isoda Koryusai (c.1740-c.1788) c.1778, woodblock print. Honolulu Academy of Arts, Gift of James A. Michener, 1970 (15,998). **Page 23:** Vintage postcard from Davis Vintage Collectibles. **Page 24:** Bottom right: Plate VIII from Holme, C.G. *Glimpses of Old Japan from Japanese Colour Prints: The Geisha*. London: The Studio Limited. **Page 24-25:** *Foreigners Enjoying Themselves in the Gankiro in the Miyosaki District in Yokohama*, woodblock print. The Metropolitan Museum of Art, Gift of Lincoln Kirstein, 1959 (JP 3264). Photograph © 1993 The Metropolitan Museum of Art. **Page 26:** *Wholesalers of cotton fabrics at Otemma Street from the series One hundred famous views of Edo* (Tokyo) c.1858 Edo (Tokyo). Colour woodcut on paper, 35.6 x 23.3 cm. Art Gallery of South Australia, Adelaide. Gift of Sir Norman Roberts, 1952. Ref: 528G113. **Page 27:** Top: *Okichi of Shimoda* © CORBIS/Art &

Archaeology; Bottom: Vintage postcards from Davis Vintage Collectibles. **Page 28:** *Japan: Autumn in Nikko* by the Japan Travel Bureau. Vintage poster courtesy of Louis Bixenman at Poster America, 138 West 18th Street, New York, NY 10011, http://www.posterfair.com **Page 29:** Plate III by Eizan from Holme, C.G. *Glimpses of Old Japan from Japanese Colour Prints: The Geisha*. London: The Studio Limited. **Page 30:** *Jokyū* (Café Girl) by Nakamura Gakuryo, from the series *Tokai josei shokufu* (Women Workers in the City), 1933. Estate of Nakamura Gakuryo, Mie Prefectural Museum of Art. **Page 31:** *L'Histoire du Costume Feminin Mondial* by Paul Louis de Giafferri from the "Illustrated Milliner," November 1928. **Page 32:** Left: *Maiko rinsen* by Tsuchida Bakusen, 1924. From the collection of The National Museum of Modern Art, Tokyo. **Page 32-33:** Upper right and clockwise paintings: (Elevator Girl, Nurse, Magician, Department Store Clerk, and Revue Girl) by Nakamura Gakuryo, from the series *Tokai josei shokufu* (Women Workers in the City), 1933. Estate of Nakamura Gakuryo, Mie Prefectural Museum of Art. **Page 34:** © 1999 Jean Francois Gate/Tony Stone Images. **Page 35:** Vintage postcard from Davis Vintage Collectibles. **Page 36:** Top and bottom: © CORBIS. **Page 37:** Vintage postcard envelope. **Page 38:** © CORBIS/Horace Bristol. **Page 39:** © CORBIS/Hulton-Deutsch Collection. **Page 40:** © CORBIS/ Horace Bristol. **Page 41:** Vintage postcard from Davis Vintage Collectibles. **Page 42:** Antique photograph circa 1870 from Rainbow Creations. **Page 43:** Top right: © Demetrio Carrasco/Tony Stone Images; Bottom right: FPG

International; Bottom middle: Antique photograph circa 1890 from Rainbow Creations. **Page 44:** Vintage postcards from Davis Vintage Collectibles. **Page 45:** Photograph courtesy of the Japan National Tourist Organization, http://www.jnto.go.jp **Page 46:** *Mokuboji bosetsu* (Evening Snow at Mokuboji) by Gototei Kunisada ga from the series *Eight Views of Edo* (Edo hakkei), circa 1820. (Rijksmuseum voor Volkenkunde, Leiden, Jan Cock Blomoff Collection. **Page 47:** Photograph courtesy of JNTO. **Page 48:** Top left and bottom right: courtesy of JNTO; Top right: FPG International. **Page 49:** © CORBIS/Horace Bristol. **Page 50:** *Fan Dancer, Country Maiden, Autumn Dancer, and the Courtesan Full Moon Blossom* by Kitagawa Utamaro (1754-1806) c.1790, woodblock print. Honolulu Academy of Arts, Gift of James A. Michener, 1970 (15,571). **Page 51:** © CORBIS/ Michael S. Yamashita. **Page 52:** Top: © CORBIS/Charles & Josette Lenars; Bottom: Vintage postcard from Davis Vintage Collectibles. **Page 53:** By Toyoharu Utagawa. Courtesy of the Freer Gallery of Art, Smithsonian Institution, Washington, D.C., 00.113, Gift of Charles Lang Freer. **Page 54:** *Yuki* (Snow) by Utagawa Fusatane (1849-1870), fan-shaped woodblock print, The Field Museum, Chicago, IL, A112637_11c. Photograph by John Weinstein. **Page 55:** Plate V by Hokkei from Holme, C.G. *Glimpses of Old Japan from Japanese Colour Prints: The Geisha*. London: The Studio Limited. **Page 56:** © CORBIS/Horace Bristol. **Page 57:** Courtesy of JNTO. **Page 58:** © Paul Chelsey/Tony Stone Images. **Page 59:** © Nicholas DeVore/Tony Stone Images.

INDEX

advertisements, 29
Akasaka, 59

Baba Akiko, 49
Brinkley, Captain Frank, 10

calligraphy, 20, 51
Chine-Jo, 59

dancing, 20, *23, 27, 43,* 47, *50,* 51, 55–57, *58–59*
danna, 44, 60, 61

Edo. *See also* Tokyo
    Fukugawa district, 49, 61
    Yoshiwara district, 16, *50,* 51
Edo period, 29, 61
Eizan, *29*
erikae o suru, 44, 60

flower arranging, 20, 60
furin, 59
furisode, 60

gei, 51–52, 60
geiko, 8
geisha, definition of, 60
Ginza, 59
Golden, Arthur, *Memoirs of a Geisha,* 9, 11–12, 31, 38, 44
Gotoba, Emperor, 16

hairdos, 21, 31, 35, 42, 60
hanamachi, 29, 44, 49, 60
hangyoku, 42, 60
haori, 11, 49, 60
Harris, Townsend, 27
Heian era, 20
Hiroshige, Ando, *12, 13, 26,* 27
Hokkei, *5*
Horikawa, Lady, 27
Hoshino Tatsuko, 44
hostesses and hostess clubs, 9, 59, 60

ikebana, 60
iki, 31, *46,* 47, 48–49, 60
iroke, 47, 60

jokyū, 30, 31, 60

Kabuki theater, *20–21,* 52, 57, 60
Kamegiku, 16
kamuro, 21, 60
kappore, 55
karyūkai, 60
Kasen, 23
kimono, 8, 9, *13, 31,* 40, 41, 42, *43, 44, 46, 47,* 48, 49, 57
Koryūsai, Isoda, *22,* 23
ko-uta, 11, 38, 42, 52, 55, 60
Kunisada, Gototei, *46,* 47
Kyoto, 8, *27,* 57, 58
    Gion district, 11–12, *13,* 29, 47, 57
    Shimabara district, 16

MacArthur, General Douglas, 39
MacLaine, Shirley, 11
Madame Butterfly (Puccini), 10
Madonna, 11
maiko, 8–9, *11, 12, 27, 32,* 41, 42, *43, 44–45, 47, 58,* 60
male *geisha,* 23, *24*
mama-san, 59, 60
Meiji period, 61
minarai, 42, 60
Mitsunoki, *14,* 15
Miyako dances, 57
mizuage, 9, 42, 58, 60
mobo, 31, 60
modan, 31
moga, 31, 60
momoware, 60
mompe, 35
Mount Fuji, *10, 12*
Murasaki Shikibu, *The Tale of Genji,* 15, 20, 29

musicianship, 15, 20, 23, *43, 51,* 52–55, *58–59*
My Geisha (film), 11

naga-uta, 55, 60
Nakamura Gakuryo, *30,* 31, *32–33*
Nikawa festival, *50,* 51
Nikko, *28,* 29
Noh theater, 16, 57, 60

obi, 39, 41, 43, 48, 49, 57, 60
oiran, 21, 23, *40, 41, 43,* 61
okāsan, 40, 41, 44, 61
Okichi of Shimoda, *27*
Okuni, 52
onēsan, 42, 61
Ono no Komachi, 12, 19
Osaka, 57
    Shimmachi district, 16
oshaku, 42, 60

patrons, 21, 35, 44, 58
Perry, Admiral Matthew C., 29
poetry, 20, 51
postcards, *11,* 29, *37*
posters, 11, 29
Puccini, Giacomo, *Madame Butterfly,* 10

Recreation and Amusement Association, 39
Ryoi, Asai, *Tales of the Floating World,* 20

saburuko, 15, 16, 61
san san kudo, 42, 61
senryū, 13, 21, 44, 48, 57, 61
sexual attitudes, 9, 10, 15, 16, 29, 31, 39, 42, 44, 58–59
shamisen, 8, *16,* 23, 47, 51, 52–55, 58, 60, 61
Shigemasa, Kitao, *2*
shikomi, 41–42, 61

shinkansen, 58, 61
shinzō, 21, 61
shirabyōshi, 15–16, 61
Shizuka, 16, 61
Shōwa period, 61
sumo wrestlers, *13*
sutorippu, 59

Taishō period, 61
Tale of Genji, The, 15, 20, 29
Tales of the Floating World, 20
tatsumi geisha, 22, 23, 61
tayū, 21, 61
tea ceremony, 20, 51
teahouses, 8, *19*
"telephone clubs," 59
Tokugawa regime, 16, 29
Tokyo, 29, 57. *See also* Edo
    Nezu district, *15*
Toyokuni, Utagawa, *20–21*
Tsuchida Bakusen, *6, 32*

ukiyo, 61
ukiyo-e prints, *12,* 21, 29, 48–49, *52–53, 54,* 61
Utamaro, Kitagawa, *50,* 51

World War II, 35–39

Yokohama
    Gankirō district, *24–25*
Yosano Akiko, 29, 39, 55
Yoshikazu, *24–25*
Yoshitoshi, *15*
Yoshitsune, 16, 61
Yoshiwara, 23
yūjo, 16, 23, 41, 48–49, 60, 61
yūkaku, 16–21, 61

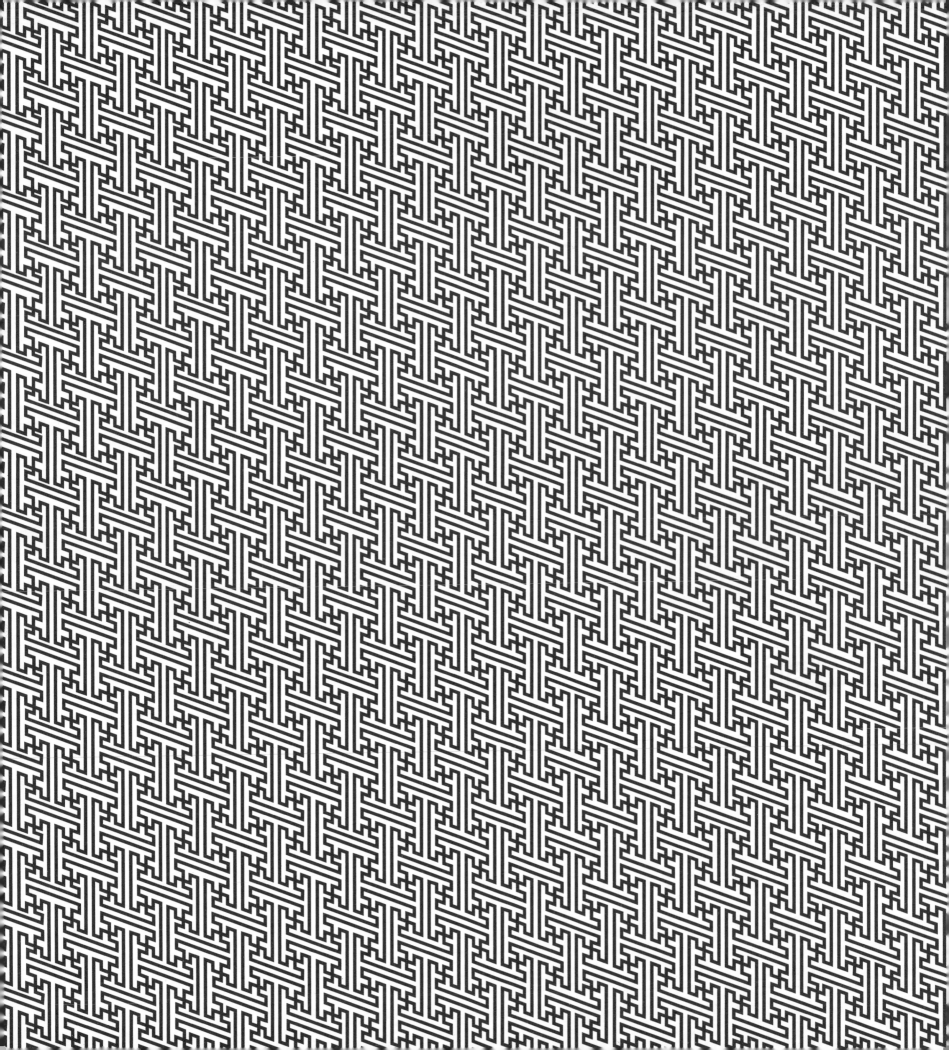